uh huh honey

red gaskell

(a compilation of kanye west's tweets featuring my illustrations)

I will work on this "book" when I feel it. When We
sit still in the mornings We get hit with so many ideas
and so many things We want to express. When I read
this tweet to myself I didn't like how much I used the
word I so I changed the I's to We's.

- @kanyewest
8:21am April 18, 2018

words by kanye west's twitter
illustrations by red

feel free to draw your own illustrations in the blank
ones or do better ones of mine

too much emphasis is put on originality. Feel free to take ideas and update them at your will all great artist take and update.

-@kanyewest

Some people have to work
within the existing consciousness
while some people can
shift the consciousness

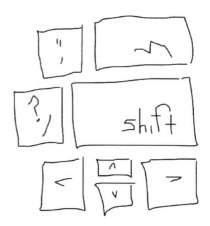

As a creative
your ideas are your
strongest form
of currency

You have to protect your ability to create at all cost

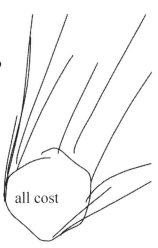

all cost

ability to create

try to avoid any contractual situation
where you are held back from your
ideas

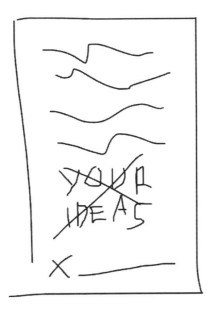

distraction is the enemy of vision

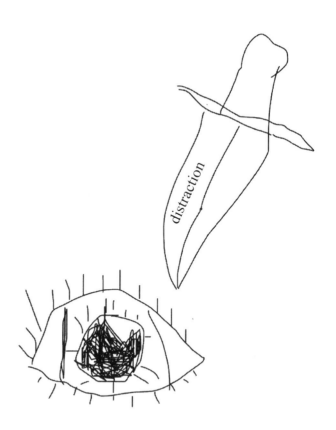

Sometimes you have to get rid of

e
 v
  e
   r
    y
     t
      h
       i
        n
         g

everything you do in life
stems from either fear or love

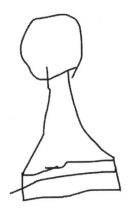

be transparent as possible. Stop setting plays. Stop playing chess with life. Make decisions based on love not fear.

trend is always late

when you first wake up don't hop right on
the phone or the internet or even speak to
anyone for even up to an hour if possible.
Just be still and enjoy your own imagination.
It's better than any movie.

You have the best ideas. Other people's opinions are usually more distractive than informative. Follow your own vision. base your actions on love. Do things you love and if you don't absolutely love something stop doing it as soon as you can.

I don't believe in the concept of an enemy. We have been conditioned to always be in competition. Stop looking for something to beat and just be. You don't have to do all the work. Once you start moving in love the universe will assist you.

You will be a drop of water with the ocean as your army. If you move out of fear than your on your own. Then it's just you and the money and the countless people you have to lie to and manipulate to build a man made path that will never lead to true happiness.

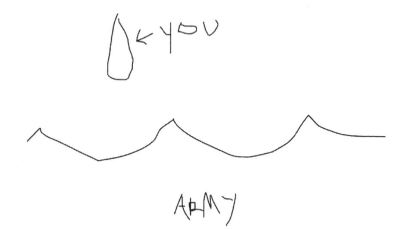

just stop lying about shit. Just stop
lying.

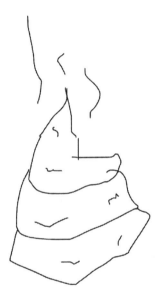

me and my friend Anthony
Schiller always ask questions
about time. Is time linear? I
recently did an interview where I
placed a high value on time. Everything means nothing until you
make it something. You are your
validator.

Be here now. Be in the moment. The now is the greatest moment of our lives and it just keeps getting better. The bad parts the boring parts the parts with high anxiety. Embrace every moment for its greatness. This is life. This is the greatest movie we will ever see.

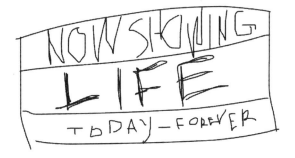

There's love stories. Pain happiness. It's 3 dementional. There's taste touch sound. It's the most entertaining for of entertainment. Just being. We believe time is a man made construct. Actually time and money are both man made currency. Because you can spend them both.

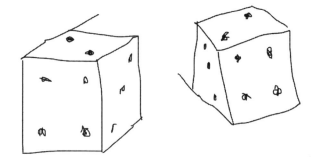

Cars have four wheels.
Hoodies have hoods.
It's amusing to me when some
one says this is an original hoodie.
Bro...
it's a hoodie

let's be less concerned with ownership
of ideas. It is important that ideas see
the light of day even if you don't get the
credit for them. Let's be less concerned
with credit awards and external
validation.

don't trade your authenticity for approval

truth is my goal. Controversy is my gym. I'll
do a hundred reps of controversy for a 6 pack
of truth

we're all servants

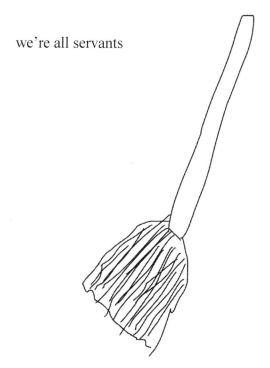

it's not where you take things from. It's where
you take them to

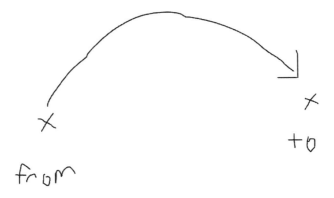

from

it's called Kids See Ghost. That's the
name of our group

Pull up in this bitch like

we need to Aman Giri the world

people are celebrating real ideas and vibe.
Not just hype

I need a water proof silk nylon as soon as possible.

all you have to be is yourself

yourself

others

I don't believe in horizontal hierarchy. If you build a ladder too high it's actually most dangerous for the people at the top.

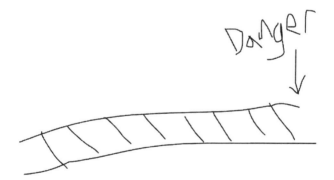

images are limitless and words aren't. Words are defined

strive for universal consciousness not
segregated consciousness

style is genderless

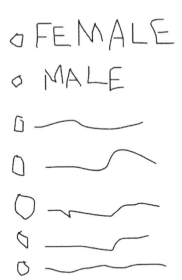

the world is our office

be fearless. Express what you feel not
what you've been programmed to think.

question everything

iterations of ideas are how culture
evolves.

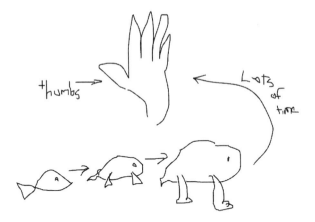

Constantly bringing up the past keeps you stuck there

author's note: hope you smiled, laughed, or at least found this entertaining

Made in the USA
San Bernardino, CA
08 May 2018